T.J. Rohleder's...

NO-PRESSURE SALES SYSTEM

How Even Quiet and Shy People Can Make a Fortune in Sales.

This book is
dedicated to my
first sales manager,
Ron Shepherd.

Direct Response Network
P.O. Box 198
Goessel, Kansas 67053-0198

FIRST EDITION

ISBN 1-933356-65-0

THINGS I WANT YOU TO READ!

INTRODUCTION

In the fall of 1983 I got a call that changed my life. It was from my friend Ron Shepherd. He had just become the manager for a store in Colorado Springs called Military TV and Stereo (MTV for short). He wanted me to move to Colorado and work in his sales department. "You'd be perfect for this!" he said "You're already a great salesman and you don't even know it! I'll teach you how to sell and you'll make a lot of money!"

Colorado Springs was six hours away. I was 23 years old and had a girlfriend that I thought I was madly in love with. Plus, all my friends were here and I didn't want to leave them. It was a big decision, but I hated my job and Ron knew it. I had been working as a welder in a factory that made mobile home frames, and hated going to work every day. Prior to that, I had dozens of meaningless, low-skilled jobs. I dropped out of school at 16 to work in the oil field in south-central Kansas and since that time, had many factory and construction jobs, all of which I hated. But these low-skilled jobs were all I could find. Ron knew all this and it took him less than an hour to convince me to take the job.

So in January of 1984, I loaded my belongings into my beat up Ford Econoline van and moved to Colorado Springs. Ron became my first sales manager and taught me how to sell. He gave me books to read. He answered all of my questions. I became dedicated to learn all I could about selling. Our store was also a training center for other new managers who would spend time at our store before setting out to manage their own. I got to know some of these people and learned all I could from them. All this became the solid foundation of my future success. And Ron was right! I did end up making a lot of money. In fact, within seven years from the time I took that sales job, I was a millionaire.

Selling changed my life. So many exciting things took place during those first seven years and the decades since. But nobody ever gets rich by themselves. I had a lot of help from many other people, including above all else my wife Eileen who also became my business partner. And yet, if it wasn't for taking that sales job and letting Ron teach me his best sales methods, none of the other great things that followed would have happened.

I've spent decades learning many different forms of sales and marketing, including how to use the power of direct response marketing to build automated systems that eliminate the need for prospecting (cold-calling), how to write ads and sales letters that let people buy without a salesperson having to talk with them (so some of our sales come through our sales team, and some come in through automation), and many other little-known methods that make selling even easier. I've devoted myself to learning as many different aspects of sales and marketing I could, including direct mail, online advertising, the process of structured selling, sales management, and more. All of this (with a lot of help from many other talented people, some who are still with me) has generated many tens of millions of dollars in sales and been extremely fulfilling.

Now I'm on a new mission to teach the best of my methods to as many other people as possible. I'm doing this for two reasons: First, it bothers me greatly that selling is not taught in school. I hate the fact that there are tens of millions of people who are like I was before I learned how to sell. These people are working in meaningless jobs and going nowhere fast, just like I was in 1983. Many of these people could become great salespeople if they had somebody to teach them how, like my friend Ron taught me.

But the whole world has changed since I went to work for Ron at that small store in Colorado Springs. And that brings me to the second reason why I wrote this book; it's the fact that the world of selling is so much different now and I want to help people understand how these changes have made selling even easier and more lucrative.

For example, because of all of these technological changes, there's no need to use the old fashioned methods of selling, such as dealing with tons of rejection and cold prospecting. Millions of salespeople are still using these antiquated methods and working way too hard for way too little money. Most of these people hate the constant prospecting and rejection they must face every day, but they don't know there's a better way. I'm on a mission to help as many of these people as possible by showing them an easier and more effective and profitable way to sell...

Are you one of these people? If so, I can help you! With my methods, you can make big money in sales with no cold calling, no dealing with tons of rejection, and no high-pressure selling. Plus, you can make money with all of my little-known sales methods without leaving home. Yes, it's true. My sales team and I stay home and sell every day and so can you! If you'd like, I can teach you how to do it with whatever you're already selling.

Look, almost everything you've been taught about selling is wrong. Especially if you learned from a sales training school or some old-school sales guru. The days of HIGH-PRESSURE and MANIPULATION are over. These old-fashioned selling methods don't work anymore. People refuse to be sold these days. They have way more natural sales resistance. Their "BS Radar" is hyper-active.

What's needed is a whole new approach to selling. A way to get people's attention and make them want to buy, but a way to make the sale without the high-pressure methods that don't work anymore.

Our NO-PRESSURE SALES SYSTEM is the only way to sell in today's world. It will change your entire approach to sales, selling, and doing business. You'll make more sales and, perhaps for the first time ever, you may actually enjoy selling!

Take a look at the final section of this book to learn more about how a Membership in our No-Pressure Sales System Coaching and Consulting Service could change your life.

Thank you for reading my book. I hope it makes a difference in your life. Selling really is the greatest professional on earth! And if you're not already involved in sales, I hope that something I say in this book, or the chance to go to work with me and my team, will become the pivotal point in your life, just like moving to Colorado Springs going to work for my friend Ron Shepherd was for me.

I look forward to hearing from you as you continue your journey to sales success, whether you continue on this path on your own, or decide to work with me. Please look over the last section of this book, where you'll find my contact information and more information on how we can work together.

Selling is manipulation.

- -

Selling is a game! It's the game of
understanding people on a very
deep level – their fears, hopes, and
desires, and then using that knowledge
to craft sales messages that go right
to the heart and soul of the prospect.

- -

Selling is an emotional experience. People buy for
emotional reasons and justify their purchase logically.

- -

Selling is finding out what people
want and letting them have it.

- -

Developing a great sales message is a process.

It takes a great deal of time, work, thinking, and
re-thinking. The best ideas develop after a great
amount of brainstorming and testing. Einstein said,
"Genius is one percent inspiration, ninety nine percent
perspiration" and that is especially true in sales.

Selling is the gentle art of
letting people have it your way.

- -

Selling is a performance: It's up to you
to create the illusion that you care more
about them than you care about yourself.
Put all the focus on them and not you.

- -

We sell solutions (people want
solutions to their pain and frustration).

- -

Timid salespeople raise skinny kids.

- -

Selling is the art of proving that what you have to offer
is worth far, far more than the money you are asking
them to give up. It is your ability to convince the prospect
that it's in their best interest to give you their money.

- -

Selling is a transference of belief and emotion.
You must be sold before you can sell it.

Don't trust your feelings.

You must talk positively to yourself and never listen to your doubts and fears. You are better, smarter and stronger than you think. So continue to do all you can to motivate, inspire, and encourage yourself.

Your feelings may try to convince you that:

- You're not improving...

- You're not going to make it....

- You don't have what it takes...

- You're not good enough....

- Everything you're doing is futile...

- You're never going to make it...

- Things are not going to work out...

- And other lies...

Most people poison themselves with negative self-talk. They sell themselves short. They put themselves down in all kinds of little ways. Don't make this mistake. Constantly remind yourself that you are better, stronger, and capable than you may feel you are and that you deserve to have the very best things that life has to offer.

Selling is an art, skill, and discipline.

- -

You must become who they need you to be.

- -

Selling is among the highest paid professions.

- -

People love to buy, but hate to be sold.
So the art of salesmanship is to sell
without them realizing they're being sold.

- -

Selling takes a few weeks to learn and a lifetime to master.

- -

Nothing happens until something is sold.
The solution to almost every business
problem is to make more sales and profits.
Because of this, the door will always be
open to the person who knows how to sell.

Take away selling: Sometimes when you hold back, it only makes them want you more.

- -

Selling is the greatest profession on earth! The fact that salespeople are not getting the respect they deserve is so wrong. Every one owes their livelihood to the people whose primary responsibility is making the cash register ring!

- -

3 reasons why people don't buy:

#1. Not interested.

#2. No money, can't afford.

#3. Don't believe you.

- -

There is no such thing as "hard sell" or "soft sell". There is only "smart sell" and "stupid sell".

You don't become a master by
learning how to do 4,000 things.
You become a master by doing
12 important things 4,000 times.

- -

Use the power of the hype! People like it. It stirs their
emotions and wakes them up! You now have their full
attention. You have broken through the clutter. Of course,
your biggest challenge (and the art behind using
hype in your sales presentation) is in the way you
hype it up, without making it sound like hype.

- -

Amateurs hope, professionals work.

- -

Marketing is a 3-step process:

#1. Attract qualified leads.

#2. Convert the highest percentage of those leads into sales.

#3. Re-sell the largest number of these customers.

Each step is distinct and sets up the next step.

"If it doesn't look like my new sales reps are going to make at least $200,000 a year within their first 6 months, I fire them!"
— George Douglas (September 22nd, 1990)

- -

Good prospects are silently begging to be led.

Whenever you are asking people for anything, always remember that you are not dealing with creatures of logic, but with creatures of emotion, creatures bristling with prejudice, and motivated by pride, greed, and fear.

- -

The #1 reason people buy almost anything and everything is because somehow they believe it will help them feel better about themselves.

Why do they buy what you sell?

It's all about psychology...
Acquiring an intimate understanding of
what makes the people in your market tick:

- What excites the people you sell to the most and why?

- What are the real reasons they buy?

- What are the offers they love the
most... Why do you think this is?

- What are they really searching for, but will never tell you?

- What are their biggest dreams and fantasies?

- What are they searching for that
even they don't understand?

The ability to understand the unconscious reasons
why your best prospects buy from you will make
you even more money. This gives you the power
to attract even more of these same types of people.
All you have to do is see and feel the world
through their eyes. This can be a great deal of fun!
Just pretend you're a psychologist and go to work
to deeply understand the people you sell to.

People buy for irrational and emotional reasons.

The best prospects are secretly searching for
"The Magic Bullet". This is the one product or service
that will solve some major problem or give them a
miracle cure! They want an instant solution to their
biggest problems. If they believe you can give this to
them, you will get their money. If they don't, you won't.

- -

Strive to develop irresistible offers.

- -

4 stages of learning something new:

#1. Unconscious incompetence –
You don't know what you don't know.

#2. Conscious incompetence – You begin to realize
and discover the things you don't know. This is the
frustration and confusion period. You're still incompetent,
but at least your eyes are beginning to open.

#3. Conscious competence – You can function in the new
area, but it's a major struggle and you're not very good.

#4. Unconscious competence – Mastery.
You have mastered the main areas and you
do great work naturally, like a duck in water!

The purpose of a good marketing system is to bring you a steady flow of qualified prospects who want what you offer. They are pre-sold. Converting large numbers of them to customers is now even easier.

If you think small, you'll stay small!

The secret to success is in these 2 questions:

#1. What exactly do you want?

#2. What price are you willing to pay to get it?

There is no such thing as non-manipulative selling.

To gain the most power, our sales messages must appear to be completely altruistic. Since the prospect only cares about themselves and "what's in it for them", everything we do must appear to be about what we can do for them.

- -

The marketplace usually responds well to clarity, certainty, and confidence; to the person who refuses to bow his head in embarrassment or humility.

- -

When a prospect says they don't have the money that means they don't have the money for you... until you prove to them that what you have for them can give them what they want.

Don't wish things were easier, wish that you were better!

- -

The key to massive productivity is to set higher goals. Commitment, deadline, responsibility and pressures are your best friend because they force you to do and be more.

- -

People want to follow the smooth and easy path that someone else has paved for them.

- -

Wants vs. Needs.

To make a good living, sell people what they need, to get rich, sell them what they want. Go beyond your product or service. Sell the dream. Sell hope for a future benefit. Sell the big promise.

The secret to making easy sales.

A great salesperson can't make anyone buy something they don't want. That's why we must use a marketing system to get prospects to 'raise their hand' and show us they're interested. This lets the prospects qualify themselves by jumping through the hoops we place in front of them.

- -

Every prospect is running around with a sign that says "Please make me feel important! Make me feel good about myself!" Do what you can to sincerely fill this strong desire they have to feel important, wanted, esteemed, admired, special and the sale is yours.

How to create an irresistible offer:

#1. A nice hook. The hook is the foundation of every offer.
It's got to sound really good or they won't bite.

#2. Pile high and deeper. "You'll get this, and this, and
this! And we'll also throw in this, if you act now."
Load it up! Make it seem like they're getting so
much for their money they can't believe it!

#3. There must be a strong reason why you are
making them such a powerful offer. The more
believable the reason, the more they'll respond.

#4. You need a firm deadline and a strong
reason why this deadline is real.

- -

Is it crazy to think that you can succeed
in the biggest possible way? Maybe!

Here's a quote from Dorothea Brande in her 1936 book
'Wake Up and Live!': "Instead of overrating our abilities,
we do not understand how great they are. Few people,
except those who are truly insane believe that they are
suited for careers that are far beyond their full powers."
So go crazy! Set goals that are higher than anything
you can imagine. Who knows, you may grow into them.
Or in an outrageous attempt to achieve these goals, you
could set off in a whole new direction that you would have
never imagined, had you not decided to think and act bigger.

Sell offers, not products or services.

An offer is made up of the greatest stuff they'll get when they give you their money. Your job is to find out what is irresistible to your prospects and let them have it.

- -

The easiest sale you'll ever make is to someone who feels bonded to you.

- -

You serve yourself best when you serve others the most.

- -

The door is always open to the person who understands how to make money. All great salespeople are extremely valuable, because we're the ones who make the cash register ring!

Your prospect is more
important than your product.

- -

Selling teaches you the true
nature of people. People reveal
themselves by the items they buy
and the actions they take. All selling
is emotional. Our sales messages tap
into emotions such as greed, vanity,
fear, laziness, pride, ego, jealousy.

- -

Greed is more powerful
than common sense.

- -

The power of empathy.

It's your ability to crawl inside the heart and mind of the
prospect and communicate directly to their emotions that
makes you a great salesperson. It's like method acting. You
know them so well that you become them! You crawl inside
their skin. You feel what they feel. You think their thoughts.

Closing the sales becomes a very
natural process when you use other
marketing methods and systems
to pre-sell the prospect.

- -

Focus on creating sales
messages with strong
emotional impact.
Prospects evaluate your
sales message emotionally
first and then intellectually.

- -

The irresistible offer.

If you had only one sales method to
rely on, it would be the irresistible offer.
Give people something they really want
and they'll come out of the woodwork like
a herd of hungry cockroaches to get it!

Making a lot of money is not
about doing what you love.
It's about finding out what
produces the biggest results
and choosing to fall in
love with those things.

- -

People buy cures, not prevention.
They'll spend their life-savings on a wild
cure, but little or nothing on prevention.

- -

Your ability to sell gives you
greater control of your life.

- -

Great products often fail because
they were not properly sold.

Most people are controlled
by their unconscious desires.
It's up to you to know what
these unconscious desires are.

Cold-calling sucks!

Whenever possible,
let the buyer feel as if
they are seeking you out,
rather than the other way.
It's all about perception.
But great marketers are
masters of altering the
perceptions of those we
want to do business with.

How to lower their sales resistance.

Just get the prospect to take an initial action.
Then lead them through a series of steps.
This lowers their sales resistance and
makes them feel as if they are in control.

- -

Your prospects don't give a damn
about you, your company, or your
products or services. They only care
about themselves. But, if you have a
system that qualifies your prospects,
you know that they do care about
owning the benefits of what you offer.
<u>This</u> <u>is</u> <u>your</u> <u>power</u>. You must build
so much value in your offers that it
breaks down their resistance to buy.

- -

Blur the lines between your work and play.

Let your marketing systems
pre-sell the prospect.
They come to your sales
reps already pre-sold.
Closing the sale becomes
a very natural progression,
because the prospect has
already taken some initial
steps to prove they're serious.
Now, even average sales
reps can close the sale.

- -

2-step marketing lets people feel that
they are the ones chasing you. You can
be very aggressive with your marketing
without appearing like you need or even
care whether they do business with you.

How to sell them without letting
them know they are being sold.

The key is to use highly emotional stories and
metaphors, analogies and concepts. When done
right, these tools can easily break down their
sales resistance. They are super powerful indirect
ways to get your sales message into their heart.

- -

The power of take-away selling.

Nothing bothers people more than giving them something
they really want and then threatening to take it away.
The more they want it, and the more they know you can
take it away, the more sales and profits you will make.

- -

Everything worthwhile is
always harder than you think.

- -

Sales and marketing is the ultimate game. This lets
you test your skills on a daily basis. Entrepreneurs
thrive on challenges! We welcome adversity. We
need new problems, challenges, and obstacles,
because without them, the game is too boring.

From the movie "Napoleon Dynamite":

"Vote for me, and all your wildest dreams will come true."

Tell them their wildest dreams
will come true if they vote for you!

- -

Formal generalized education sucks. The only thing that's important is specialized knowledge and experience that's focused in a very specific direction.

- -

Your job is to convince the highest qualified prospective buyer that:

#1. You know more than they do.

#2. You are among the few who
can give them what they want.

#3. Your intentions are honorable and
you have their best interests at heart.

Nothing sells itself. This is a stupid myth. Behind every great sales campaign are a lot of people and other things that are making it happen.

- -

Using fear:

"In order to sell insurance, the prospect must see the hearse backed up to his door, feel the cold breath of the Grim Reaper raising the hairs on the back of his neck, and hear the death rattle in his chest." — Cavett Robert

- -

Sell money at a discount.

Strive to sell dollars for dimes. Your primary goal is to prove that what you offer will make them money, not cost them money. In fact, they'll lose money by not doing business with you.

The power of comparisons.

You can never know the true value of something until and unless you compare it with something else. So find as many ways as possible to associate yourself, your company, and your products and services with other items that have the greatest value in the minds and hearts of the people you sell to.

- -

If your enthusiasm is gone, it's because you failed to feed it.

- -

The power of 2-step marketing.

The magic behind this form of marketing is the fact that makes the prospect or customer feel they are choosing you. They feel as if they are the one who is in control and has the power. They feel less threatened, and this is your gateway to the sale.

Great salespeople see
everything through the eyes
of their customers.

- -

Build your marketing system to:

#1. Attract the best prospects.

#2. Proves that you have many compelling
advantages over all the rest.

#3. Establish your true value.

#4. Sell them on your unique selling proposition.

#5. Makes them an in irresistible offer.

Closing the sale is easy when your
marketing system does these five things.

- -

The job of the first sale is
to whet their appetite and
make them hungry for more!

People hate to be sold, but love to be entertained.

The most successful salespeople know
how to reach and move people emotionally.
They fire people up and inspire them.
They get people excited! They have great
energy and enthusiasm. They pump a lot of
passion into what they say. They're on fire!

For years I had a sign on my wall from the movie,
"Leap of Faith", where Steve Martin's character shouts:
"Let's give those empty lives a little meaning!" I hung
that quote right above the place where I recorded the
sales presentations that went out to my prospects
and customers. I also had signs that said:
"Give it everything you've got!" and one word
quotes like "Perform!" and other motivational
sayings to remind myself to pump up the passion!
I still have handwritten signs up on my wall.

Entertaining prospects and buyers is important because
bored people don't buy. Neither do skeptical people.
These people don't trust you and are sick and tired of
the same old sales presentations. You must deviate from
the script, so you can shake them up to wake them up!
Selling is a performance and your best prospects want
to be entertained. So jazz it up! Say and do things that
make your sales presentation more fun and interesting.
Be as enthusiastic as you can and make them feel it!

Selling is the most important
profession on earth.

Nothing happens until something is sold. Most companies
depend on those of us who are most responsible for making
the cash register ring. We are not more important than
the rest of the staff, it's just that we are the ones who make
their jobs possible! (Unless they work for the government
or giant corporation that is in bed with the government.)

- -

Think of your offer as if it
were "the product" you sell.

- -

Great premiums drive the sale.

Make your bonuses so attractive and valuable
that people are willing to buy your product
or service just because they want them.

- -

We are all self-made,
but only the successful
will admit it.

Only an idiot would ask someone to marry them on the 1st or 2nd date. First, you win their trust, love, and respect. You do all you can to let them know who you are and why you are the one for them. Then and only then do you even think of asking for their hand in marriage. Same in business. The prospect must be courted!

- -

Only results count.

In the 1950s Rosser Reeves created what he called "A hard-sell advertisement" to cut through the clutter and drive his sales message home. It worked. Reeves created several hard-sell commercials for Anacin that he called "the most hated commercials in the history of advertising." But in 18 months they raised Anacin sales from $18 million to $54 million. Lesson: It doesn't matter who you piss off, it only matters who you sell!

It's about them, not you.

The foundation behind all great sales
messages is empathy. It's your ability
to understand what they want the
most and how to give it to them that
matters most. It's how well you are able
to connect with them, build strong
bonds, and let them know you truly
care. And since they're giving you
their money, you should strive to care
about them as much as possible!

- -

From Norman Vincent Peale's book
"Enthusiasm Makes the Difference".

"The greatest sales job you'll ever have is to
sell yourself on yourself. To bring yourself to an
enthusiastic acceptance of yourself is one of the
biggest feats of all. How to make yourself believe
in yourself, your abilities, talents, capacities,
requires the most enthusiastic persuasion."

Selling gets easier after your 1,000th sales pitch.

- -

Never listen to your doubts and fears. Talk positively to yourself and never listen to yourself.

Fake it until you make it. Being enthusiastic during your sales presentation will help you in the beginning, before you develop your sales skills.

- -

The battle for the sale.

Because selling is a performance, it's all about control and power. Power is your ability to act. It's exercising your total control over something. In every selling situation, someone is in control. It's either you or them. They're trying to do all they can to hold onto their money and you're trying to do all you can, short of physical violence or downright dishonesty, to get it! In every battle there can be only one winner. Your mission is to make sure that you are the one who wins.

What you really sell.

What your customers really want and what you sell
can be as different as night and day, and yet it's
up to you to understand this and then close the gap.

For example: I've been selling business opportunities since
1988, but what my customers really want is a sure-fire
investment opportunity. In a perfect world, they're searching
for a very small investment that can turn into a huge fortune!
The problem is, I don't sell investments. So my job is to find
as many ways as possible to make each business opportunity
feel less like a business and more like an investment.

You must do things like this, too. It all starts
with spending a lot of time thinking about
your best prospects and customers:

- Why do they buy the things you sell?

- What do they really want?

- What is the desire behind their desire?

- In a perfect world, if you could give them
  anything they wanted, what would it be?

Once you have some of these answers, you can
create new product and service combinations
that do a better job of filling these emotional wants
in a more powerful way than your competition.

The "Game Theory" of sales.

The study of "Game Theory" is the latest buzz of the academic community. The concept is simple: <u>Put yourself into a position that you don't want to be in and then rescue yourself</u>. In the process of doing this, you'll discover many interesting things. When I first read about this I said to myself: "This is what all great entrepreneurs have been doing for thousands of years!" It's true. We force ourselves to tap into parts of ourselves that we don't normally reach by constantly biting off way more than we can chew. We back ourselves into corners and fight our way out!

- -

Your ability to influence others is your greatest skill.

- -

Empathy may be the most important marketing principle.

As the old adage says: "If you're going to sell something that Betty buys, you've got to see things through Betty's eyes!" Your prospects and customers must believe that you understand their problems and pain and feel many of the same things they feel. Once they believe this, they will be ready to do business with you.

"Certainty is hugely seductive."
— Anthony Starr

People are desperately seeking
certainty in an uncertain world.
They want to be near someone who
they feel has figured it all out and
will take care of them. The strongest
leaders project total confidence.
This is the source of the magnetic
pull they have over their followers.

- -

They all want something new.

One of our best-pulling sales letters has a headline
in 72-point type that says, "NEW!" That's it. Just this
simple three-letter word. And yet people go crazy over
anything that appears to be new! They think if it's new,
it might be better. Your job is to keep giving them the
same old stuff they want the most, with a thin layer
of something unique, so now it can be sold as new.

Human nature never changes.

Thousands of years ago Socrates said:

"Few love what they may have."

What we do love or desire the most will
always be slightly out of reach. People
can always be led to believe that something
they'll get is better than what they already have.

- -

Be thankful for your burdens.

"If it were not for the things
that go wrong in your work,
for the difficult people you have
to deal with, for the burden of the
decisions you have to make, and
for the responsibility you carry,
a lesser person could do your job
at about half of what you make."
— Nido R. Quebein

A secret from a Nobel Prize winner:

Eric Hoffers' classic book "The True Believer" begins with these words: "It all starts with a frustrated person." This is very important, because the people who buy the most are the ones who are the most unhappy or frustrated (there are exceptions, but they are few). You must realize that it is the tremendous pain that people feel creates the internal pressures that buying your type of product or service will solve (or can be made to feel it will). It's up to you to put them in touch with their pain, stir up these emotions, and then offer your product or service as the ultimate solution!

NOTE: According to Kurt Mortensen, studies show that as many as two-thirds of all Americans suffer from some degree of low self-esteem. This is great news for you, because to suffer from low self-esteem is directly related to feeling frustrated and unhappy. These are the internal pressures that drive people to buy.

- -

Sell the unfamiliar by linking it to what they already know, understand, and value.

- -

Keep searching for faster, simpler, and easier ways to do all of the most important things you must do to make the most money.

A good marketing system is like a money machine.

Your marketing system will generate leads and close sales for you automatically. It is your well-oiled money-machine that cranks out huge sums of automatic cash for you at the push of a button. This entire system is developed to take the new person through all of these stages:

#1. Suspect to prospect.

#2. Prospect to buyer.

#3. Buyer to customer.

#4. Customer to repeat customer.

#5. Repeat customer to raving fan.

- -

"Everything you want is on the other side of your comfort zone."
— Ted Ciuba

The future of selling.

The days of being dependent upon one media or one way of selling are over. The future will require a sophisticated sales and marketing process, to attract and re-sell the largest number of the best prospects and customers. Talented salespeople will always be a vital part of this process. These salespeople will help to make the initial sale and set the stage for all future sales.

- -

People are searching for something real.

All of us are searching for something real in a phony world. So let the people you sell to see your imperfections. This will turn many people off, but as long as your offer is targeted to the best prospects, you'll still break through the thick layers of skepticism and penetrate that part of them that makes them want to buy from you.

Your market comes first.

The market you sell to is far more important than the products and services you sell. In fact, the secret to developing the hottest-selling products and services is to stay focused on the various ways you can solve the biggest problems that the best prospective buyers face. Make a detailed list of these problems. Put yourself in the shoes of the best prospects. Then develop newer and better products and services that are designed to solve the biggest problems these people face and gives them more of what they want the most. Then create your marketing messages to let these people clearly understand how you can solve their biggest problems.

Selling is a process, not an event.

There's a process you must take every prospect
through, to get them to the point where they're
ready to buy. The best way to take them through
this process is by developing a complete marketing
system that does all of the pre-selling for you.

Pain is a much bigger
motivator than pleasure.

Nothing kills a sale faster
than a desperate salesperson.

People smell desperation like a
dog smells fear. Never let them see
you sweat! Get your head together
before each sales presentation.
Make sure you're confident and
strong before you open your mouth.

Cold calling is a stupid way to sell.

- -

Your real power comes from developing your confidence, certainty and the way you carry yourself.

The things you say to yourself about yourself and what you believe to be true about you are the most important things. Work on the way you see, think and feel about yourself; the way you project yourself. You must strive to believe in yourself in the fullest way. You must be 100% sold on you, what you do, and the value you bring to the table. The more you do this, the more power, influence, and money you'll have.

The power of
2-step marketing.

A prospect who comes to you presold is
much more qualified and better in every way
than anyone you could ever approach yourself.
So stop chasing cold prospects and start letting
the hot prospects feel as if they are chasing you.

By using a 2-step marketing system, you
are making them think and feel as if it was
their decision to come to you. This helps to
create the illusion that they are in control.

- -

The alternative sales close is the only
closing technique you have to master.

It is very uncomfortable to say "no" to a choice of
two or more options. This is especially true when
you know the prospect has a serious interest in both
options. When that happens, the sale is almost
guaranteed! In a face-to-face selling situation,
you can see the prospect's pain when you ask
them which choice they want. Some turn red,
and if you don't blink, some will even sweat!

How to get more power and leverage over your target market.

One of the most successful business and marketing coaches, says: "You must believe you are superior to your clients and carry that attitude with you whenever you are around them. Otherwise, they won't respect you." I was sitting in the back of the room when she said this, immediately wrote it down and couldn't get it out of my head. This is a bold and controversial statement. But if there is one quality many super-successful people seem to have, it's an air of superiority. This is what attracts and repels people to them.

So what's the difference between an egotist and a person who is really superior? It's the way you answer these questions:

- Do you really have the goods?

- Have you paid the price?

- Have you done something excellent?

Many people feel superior without having done anything extraordinary. How crazy is that? But someone who has paid the price and done amazing things that are far beyond the average Joe has earned the right to think, feel, and carry themselves with an air of quiet confidence and superiority.

Can you fake enthusiasm?

Yes, just talk 3 times faster. People will think and feel that you are enthusiastic. Plus, once you do this for awhile, you won't be faking it any more!

- -

Having money solves
the problems that not
having money creates!

- -

Position yourself as the expert.

People are silently begging for someone
to tell them what to do. They need
you to be the expert and take the lead.
Like any good expert, you must be
the one who knows best, not them.
People want to do business with
confident professionals who tell them
exactly what to do and how to do it.

You are your greatest sale.

Most people are waiting for someone else to appoint or anoint them. That's bullshit! You have to be the one who gives yourself your own gold stars. You are the one who must appoint and anoint yourself. You must be 100% sold on the most important aspects of who you are and the direction you're headed before you can persuade the right people to come along for the ride. You must develop a solid belief in your own importance and everything that make you unique and special.

If you're not sold on these things, nobody else will be.

It starts with you. Sell yourself on the fact that you really can get all of the greatest things that life has to offer. The more you believe in yourself, your ideas, your goals, dreams, and desires, your direction in life, the more you'll also convince other people to follow you.

Everyone wants to be a vital part of a winning team. We all want to get in on the action and go with the people who can take us someplace exciting! We're attracted to the person who makes us feel great about ourselves. We want to be with someone who's passionate and enthusiastic! We love to be around someone who helps us believe in ourselves and helps us realize our own unique qualities. We all want to bask in the sunshine of a passionate person who's totally alive! But none of these things will happen by accident, it's up to you to make them happen. Start doing it today!

The FUD Factor kills more sales than anything else.

FUD is an acronym for Fear, Uncertainty, and Doubt. Every prospective buyer has these 3 things even if they never mention it. It's up to you to be aware of these destructive negative emotions and develop the right selling messages to overcome them.

The minds of the average prospect are so filled with fear, uncertainty, and doubt that it's amazing most salespeople can't see it! So let me drive this point home: The people you sell to don't trust you. The only thing they care about is themselves and what they can be led to believe that you and your product or service will do to make their lives better.

- -

You're never become a professional salesperson until you've endured a number of really bad selling situations.

What matters most is how you walk through the fire. You must willingly put yourself through as many "bad" situations as possible to develop your skills. Almost all of us hate the most difficult periods, and yet these are the times of our greatest growth. Working through these terrible times in the most positive way you can will make you stronger and wiser. It's a major secret to becoming all you can be.

Agree with every objection.

This will shock them. One minute they're bracing themselves for your response to their objection, and the next minute you have caught them off guard. Now you have them exactly where you want them! The power has shifted. Now you have enough control to hammer a wedge into their sales resistance. Just find a very creative way to flip their objection around and use it against them. For example, if they say, "This is too expensive!" you agree with them and say, "You're right, it is too expensive!" Now they don't know what to say. Then all you have to do is pause for as long as you can and say: "At least it is too expensive when you compare it with all of those cheaper programs. But, there's only one problem, those programs do not work and you know it! (Then get them to agree with you about this statement.) But this is not like those programs! Here's why..." With this sales pitch, you can begin to compare it with something much more expensive and start the process of proving that what you have is actually quite affordable.

Can you see how this works? Good! If they say, "I don't have the money" or "I can't afford it" you pause and say, "Of course you can't afford it! Who can? That's what we have banks, or credit cards or our payment plan for!" Salespeople who approach objections this way have a lot more confidence and power. They even encourage objections!

Yes, selling is hard, but you can do hard things.

The things that are most difficult are also the things that challenge us the most. They force us to grow and develop our skills. They stretch us. They push us beyond our self-imposed limits. They cause us to become all we are capable of being.

- -

Adversity is a major motivator.

The secret is to re-channel all of the negative energy around you. Do this and the people who criticize you can also be the fuel to your fire. The more they tell you that you can't do something, the more motivated you will be to prove them wrong!

- -

Nothing sells like total enthusiasm and confidence.

Wisdom from Claude Hopkins:

"I created sensations and presented enticing ideas. I did not say, 'Buy my brand instead of the other fellows.' I offered them inducements which naturally led them to buy."

The key to using this principle is to stop selling products and services and start selling offers. Think of all the ways you can bundle whatever you're selling into some kind of irresistible package.

What do people really want?

That's easy: They want the biggest and most exciting results in the fastest time and for the smallest investment of money and effort. Find the ultimate way to give these things to them and watch your sales soar!

Most people settle for too little and give up way too fast.

Everything you do should be connected
with one or more of your main goals.

- -

The buyer as a child king.

More choices make the average
customer feel more empowered. Many
are like child kings who attempt to
impose their rules on us. This is good
and bad. The good part is the fact that
there is little guessing about what people
really want. We have enough extremely
vocal customers who are happy to tell
us exactly what they like and dislike...
all we have to do is follow their lead!
This takes out the guesswork over which
way the market is headed or what's most
important to the people we sell to. The
bad news is the fact that many of the
people we do business with don't ask us
to do things for them, they demand it.

"Sometimes you have to exaggerate things, to get people to see the truth!" From the movie "She Devil".

- -

The secret of blocking your time.

You can do almost anything for 30 to 45 minutes at a time. This lets you start and work on the huge and frustrating jobs you've been avoiding. Now all you have to do is go at it for small blocks of time! You don't have to deal with the pressure of finishing each project or figuring everything out. Your only problem is figuring out what to do for the next 30 minutes. What a load of pressure that removes. Try this, it works! You'll end up getting more done, everything you do will be better, and you'll enjoy it more because now it's much more of a game and not work.

The power of the upsell.

People always want more of whatever they bought before. The best upsell opportunities will always be when you can give your customers something that's very closely related to what they have already bought.

- -

Find positive meaning in doing the hardest things.

"To suffer is to feel alive!" Christie Aschwanden, in the April 2009 Runners World Magazine. This quote came from a great article that was written about these crazy ultra marathon runners who run 100 miles or more at a time over the most terrible conditions. They feel the pain and it makes them feel totally alive. Well, as salespeople, we have our own pain, and we must feel totally alive as we go through it! It's easier said, then done, but the more you push yourself, the more you find out what you are truly capable of, and it's always a lot more than you think.

Being a great salesperson and being a great sales manager are two entirely different things.

Magic Johnson was a dynamic basketball player with a shining career. But he failed miserably as a coach. He lasted 18 games with a 5 wins and 13 losses record before he finally quit. Managing requires a whole different set of skills, this is especially true when it comes to managing salespeople. Salespeople are like beautiful horses; they get easily rattled. A good sales manager must understand every aspect of their companies sales and marketing process and enjoy teaching it to others and watching them succeed.

Great salespeople love objections.

However, those of us who are smart have developed
a marketing system that answers the majority of
these objections, before we get on the phone or
spend time face-to-face with the prospective buyer.

- -

Enlightened selfishness.

It's in our nature to be selfish. We can't help it.
We're all looking out for ourselves in some way.
Our survival depends on it. But the wisest people
have discovered that the ultimate way to survive
is by teaming up with a group of like-minded
individuals. The whole idea behind enlightened
selfishness is very simple: "I win by helping you
win!" As long as we are working together and
moving forward in the same direction, then we
can both get what we want faster and easier!
Zig Ziglar said it best: "You can have anything
you want by helping enough other people get
what they want!" That great quote was printed
on the back cover of our first book. It's been
our success mantra ever since. It should be your
success mantra, too. So here's the burning question:
What are you doing right now to give as many
other people the things they want the most?

The best things are the ones
that challenge you the most.

- -

Everyone is capable of doing far more
than they realize. They simply are
not demanding more of themselves.
They settle for less. They become a
slave to the comforts and securities of life.
They never go past their comfort zones and –
if they do – it's never far or for long enough.

- -

Success comes
from self-discipline.

So does real self-esteem. Those who
want more self-esteem must do more
esteem-building activities more often.
Self-discipline is all about forcing
yourself to do the most important
things you know you must do
(but often don't feel like doing).

The power of negative thinking:

The best way I know of to gain a deep
understanding of something is to look at it
through the eyes of a person who is totally jaded.

- -

What they really
want is a miracle!

If you tell people who want to lose
weight to control their calorie intake
and do a little moderate exercise on a
regular basis, there's nothing left to sell.
Besides, that's not what people want.
They're looking for magical cures that
provide instant results, with no effort.
They want a miraculous way to eat
more food, do less exercise and still
lose weight. Find a believable way to
promise them something close to that
and they'll gladly give you their money!

Being too obvious in your sales
pitch will raise suspicion.

Here are 6 ways to sell
without being too obvious:

#1. People love new trends, so frame what
you're selling as part of a new trend.

#2. To entice the very best buyers out of their
shell, strive to become more like them.

#3. Stories and analogies let you sell, without people
realizing it. People love and remember good stories.
Facts presented alone will not persuade as well as the
right stories. With this method, your sales message
goes under the radar of their sales resistance. The right
stories create attention and involvement with your audience.
The more you do to tie your story in with the key benefits
of what you're selling, the more persuasive you will be.

#4. The less you seem to need the prospects business,
the more likely they'll be drawn to you.

#5. Lift your prospects thoughts into the clouds and
they'll relax. Their defenses will come down,
and it will be so much easier to make the sale.
Your words will become a kind of elevating drug.

#6. Those who are chasing don't get chased.
So run until they catch you!

How do deal with rejection.

Getting a little rejection is a part of our profession.
You can't take it personally. Your mantra should be:
"Some will, some won't. So what? Who's next?"

- -

They must pay before
they pay attention!

Only those who pay you money are worthy of your time
and attention. Free takers end up becoming freeloaders.
Make them pay you first. Don't ever consider someone
a good prospect until they have given you some money.
You must refuse to spend any significant time or money
with any prospect until and unless they have already
paid you something. Are there other ways you can qualify
a prospect? YES. But money is the surest way to tell
if someone is serious or not. When people pay, they
pay attention! This is a major involvement device that
will quickly show you who your very best prospects are.

- -

Sell your product/service against other items that
are loaded with problems. This lets you talk about
the problem and make them feel the pain they've
experienced with these problems. This makes
them more interested in the results you offer.

If your sales
are sluggish...

#1. It means you're not working hard enough.

#2. Your belief in what you're
selling is not strong enough.

#3. You're not as committed as you should be.

#4. You're not putting enough of
yourself into the selling process.

How you react to the hard times reveals your true character.
So take full responsibility and blame yourself for any
poor results you go through. Accept the fact that
it's your fault if your sales are sluggish. By taking
the blame, you also take the responsibility and
power to do the things that will turn it all around.

So what if the problem is not your fault? Should you still
blame yourself? Yes! Because even if you didn't cause the
situation, you can still be responsible for the actions you
have to take to get out of the mess. There's something,
or many things, you could do, but you can't see or do any
of these things if you act like a big baby and continue to
cry about the problem. Instead, accept the problem, then
take full responsibility for the solution. Only then will you
be ready, willing and able to correct the problems above.

From Elijah Woods' character in the
movie, "Green Street Hooligans":

"You don't feel alive unless you're pushing yourself as far as you can go!"

Every true entrepreneur can relate strongly to that one!

- -

All doors are open to you, once you understand and get good at selling.

- -

More reasons a
highly qualified
prospect won't buy:

#1. They don't believe you or your claims.

#2. They doubt if this will work for them.

#3. They fear they may be making a mistake.

Understand this: Fear of loss is greater than the desire for gain.
The average prospect is more afraid then you can imagine.
You must be bold and clear about all the ways you're
stacking all the chips on their side of the table and not yours.

The ultimate confidence booster.

Become really good at something the world greatly values. This is not only your meal ticket for life, but it's also an amazing confidence booster! Becoming really great at selling can take years of hard disciplined work, but it will build your confidence like nothing else.

- -

Certainty is a major attractor factor.

People want to feel total certain. It's up to you to make them feel this way. How? By feeling it yourself first. Those who are possessed with extremely strong beliefs and can passionately communicate them to others have amazing power. John Wesley, Founder of the Methodist Church, said: "I catch myself on fire and they come to watch me burn!" Your prospective buyers want to see you burn! They want to feel the heat of your passion!

There is no one way to sell; there are thousands.

You learn a little from everyone, combine it with your experience, and adapt it to your personality and your style. And yet, success leaves clues. The best salespeople are always the ones with the very best prospect and product knowledge, and who consistently give the best service.

- -

Stories Sell.

Stories help you make the sale when nothing else will. You must create powerful stories that captivate the people in your target market. These are stories about you, your company, or your products or services. Choose the right stories. They must sound real, be believable and highly emotional. There should be some kind of drama or unique idea or a perceived benefit or promise. The best stories follow a simple 'before and after' format; the story tells about the problem and introduces the solution. The prospects put themselves into this kind of story and are sold!

Happiness is a never-ending stream of positive cash-flow!

- -

Why hype it up?

We use hype and bold promises to break through the clutter of the thousands of advertising and marketing messages that are begging for our prospects attention.

People are tuned out. They have a tremendous resistance against our sales messages. The only way to get through is to go "over-the-top" and be as dramatic as possible. You must have a marketing system that does something dramatic to wake them up! This will break through their zombie-like fog, pre-sell them, and prepare them to listen to your entire sales pitch.

- -

Feeling bad about yourself for even one minute is a crime against yourself. Remind yourself that you are better than you think you are. Focus on your top 5 biggest past successes and the 5 things you have to be the most grateful for.

The only purpose of your first sale is
to build a relationship with the new
customer and get the next sale.

- -

When selling, stories can be used to...

- Get people's attention and interest.

- Get them to like, trust and identify with you.

- Make them want to know more.

- Get them excited!

- Sell without them realizing they've been sold.

- Lower their sales resistance.

- Let them get to know you and make
them feel that you are a good person
who sincerely wants to help them.

- Make complicated ideas easy to understand.

- Break their negative and fearful state of
mind and get them excited, positive, and
receptive to whatever you're selling.

- Make them want to take action!

The heart comes before the head.
You win your prospective buyers heart
first and then you'll win their business.

- -

Turn every objection into a powerful
reason why they should buy.

- -

Telling a good story that's tied to what you sell let's
you take control the situation. People who hear your
story can go from cold to hot very fast! One minute
they're bored, skeptical, half-asleep, arms folded,
lethargic, and now (assuming you tell the right
story in the right way) they're alert and ready to buy!

- -

Most people can come up with enough
money to buy something they really want.

People who say they can't afford it are usually lying. Most
people always seem to find the money to do what they want.
When they say they "don't have the money", what they mean
is "I don't have the money for you, until you prove that what
you have is worth much more than you're asking for in return!"

Become an expert.

The more you do to position yourself as someone of authority, the more leverage you'll have to persuade people to do things your way. We are unconsciously searching for someone who knows more than we do. This is especially true whenever we are forced with a great deal of uncertainty.

So how do you become an expert? Simple: First, act the part. Second, consider publishing your own books, reports, and audio programs. Consider holding seminars, webinars, and workshops. How can anyone claim to be an expert if they refuse to do any of these things? They can't, and you know it.

The more you can do to position yourself as an expert, the more money you will make:

- You will have celebrity-like power that draws people to you.

- You'll make more of the best people want to do business with you.

- All of your sales will come easier.

- The best people will be happier to pay you larger amounts of money.

All of the other persuasion techniques work so much better when your prospects perceive you as an expert. People will take you more seriously. They'll feel good about doing business with you and you'll have far more influence over them.

They say the word "FREE" is the most powerful word in the English language because it stimulates their emotions of greed... But the other 4-letter word that works just as well in some markets is "HELP!" People buy results.

And in some markets, the average prospect is in so much pain, that all they want is someone who can help them do what they want, but feel they are unable to do themselves. The salesperson who can help them the most will get their business.

- -

The delay of a sale is usually the death of a sale. Create a great deal of urgency, to make them want to take action now!

- -

Why don't they teach sales in school?

The fact that most people can't sell is sad. Salesmanship should be a required course from K to 12th grade and beyond. This should be a major part of every child's education, with advanced courses taught in college. Why this doesn't happen is a great mystery. I spend a lot of time thinking about how different our world would be if kids were taught about the supreme value of salesmanship.

The power of indirect selling.

Many prospects won't listen to what you say because:

#1. They know you're trying to get their money.

#2. They're on guard and fighting hard to keep their money.

#3. They don't believe you or, at least, they know that everything you say has a spin on it.

#4. They're bored!

Because of these things, a standard benefit-driven sales message won't make an impact. The prospect is fighting to stay in control. And the more you let them have control, the less sales you'll make. You must do something totally different: You must do something unique that wakes them up, and lets you take control of the selling situation. That's what indirect selling does.

With this aspect of selling, you're spicing up your sales presentation with all kinds of stories, metaphors, and analogies. This gets the buyer to become interested and listen. You're giving them something they didn't expect. This will separate you from all of the other salespeople. It lets you take control of the situation and makes them drop their guard and want to know more.

Sell yourself first and most.

Think it bigger and see it simpler than ever before. Be 100% sold on what you're doing and 100% committed. Enthusiasm is a skill. Being totally enthusiastic will help you get through the major obstacles that stop others. Remember this acronym: The "IASM" at the end of enthusiasm stands for "I Am Sold Myself!" Being 100% sold on anything requires time, work, energy, and lots of thinking. You must have many references to support your belief. The more references you have, the stronger your belief will be, and the more power you will have.

- -

More reasons why people won't give you their money:

#1. They don't think they have a real need for what you sell.

#2. They don't think it will work for them.

#3. They don't trust you, your company, or your offer.

#4. They do not see the value.

#5. Fear in all forms: of losing their money, of losing their self-respect, of being cheated, etc.

The ultimate sales mantra:

"Some will, some won't.
So what? Who's next?"

My most important secret:

Having an intimate knowledge of the type of people you sell to (and how you can give them what they want the most) is more important than all of the other sales and marketing ideas... combined! Strive to know these things:

1. Who are the best customers you want to attract and retain?

2. What do they want the most and how can you give it to them in the biggest and boldest way? And...

3. How can you reach them in the most effective way (to make an initial low cost sale) and then get them to re-buy as fast as possible?

The right answers to these 3 questions helped my wife and I bring in over $10,000,000 in sales in our first five years. Answer them correctly and they could help you make your fortune, too.

What people really want is a
"one-size-fits-all" solution.

* They're searching for easy answers and instant solutions.

* Many want someone else to do it all for them.

* They want someone to take away their pain and risk.

- -

Blur the lines between your work and play. Money
and fun really can mix! You must teach yourself how
to enjoy the activities that bring you the most money.

- -

How to make people want
to give you more money.

The high prices you want to charge will always
be a major problem unless the best buyers believe
that you are different and better than everyone else.
You must differentiate in ways that matter most to
your target market. It's up to you to make people
want to spend more of their hard-earned money
with you. Educate them on the greatest reasons
why it's in their best interest to keep giving
you even larger amounts of their money.

Marketing is knowing what the people you
sell to want the most and giving it to them
in a bigger and better way than anyone else.

- -

Sincerity.

Here's a great quote from marketing legend, Bruce Barton:

"The essential element in personal magnetism
is a consuming sincerity, an overwhelming faith
in the importance of the work one has to do."

Bruce was right; sincerity and empathy are two
of the greatest marketing principles you'll ever use.
Why? Because the best prospects want to trust you,
but they're so afraid. When you are sincere and
empathetic, you break down the walls of resistance
and make them want to listen to what you have to say.

To be sincere is to be honest about what you have to offer.
It means you are candid, plain speaking, natural and
unassuming. To be empathetic is to connect very deeply
with the people you sell to. It's your ability to identify
with them, to understand their biggest problems,
to give them the feeling that you understand
them and are looking out for their best interests.

"I lied to you because it was in your best interest."

From an actual conversation with
a close family member I can't name!

- -

A 4-step formula to maximize profitability:

#1. Attract – #2. Convert – #3. Upgrade – #4. Expand

It's this simple...

Step #1. Attract the right prospects. These are the people
who are most likely to want what you have and give you the
largest amount of money for the longest period of time.

Step #2. Convert the largest number
of these people into first-time buyers.

Step #3. Upgrade them by selling them as many
related products and services, as fast as you can.

Step #4. Then expand the relationship with these customers
for as long as possible! Stay in close touch with them.
Build strong bonds of friendship. Sell them as many
different related products and services as possible for as
long as you can. Strive to create a lifetime of never-ending
revenue from all of the repeat business they do with you.

A good salesperson never has to
worry about their financial future.

- -

The game of sales and marketing.

It's all about trying to figure out what the
best buyers in your market really want
and how you can give them more of it:

- What gets them most excited?

- What they're spending their money on right now?

- How can you give them what they want in
a bigger and better way than anyone else?

- What are they really searching for that causes them
to buy the kinds of products and services you sell?

Sales and marketing is giving people what they really
want in the biggest, best and boldest way. It's filling their
unfulfilled wants, if only for a moment. It's understanding
all of the emotional forces that cause them to continue to
spend their money on the types of things you sell. What
are these strong emotional forces that cause them to buy
what you sell? It's a great game to figure all of this out!
The answer to these questions are different for each market.
But once you discover these things, you can make huge
profits by re-selling them a never-ending supply of it!

The five P's of success:

#1. Psyche – You will never achieve your goals, until you firmly believe you can. The right psyche is all about knowing exactly what you want, having a solid plan to get it, and never letting anything stop you!

#2. Persistence – Successful people will not be stopped! You can knock them down 19 times and they'll get back up a 20th time. And if they can't get back up, they'll start kicking and biting. They never let the obstacles take their eyes off their goals.

#3. Personal Development – Successful people work harder on themselves than they do on their profession. All of us have huge libraries and we use them. We are constantly learning more and developing our greatest skills.

#4. Passion! Your passion is a combination of your belief, enthusiasm, and emotion. Everyone loves a passionate person. This is the key to winning their hearts and minds.

#5. Persuasion – The most persuasive people are those who can make people love to do what they want them to do. Your ability to persuade will draw the right people and circumstances to you. People will be standing in line with money in hand!

Add it up and you'll see: Having all five of these things gives you the awesome power you need to be, do, and have everything you want.

Selfishness.

When it comes to spending money,
all people care about is, "What's in it for me?"
So consider everything from their perspective.
Keep asking yourself, "What are all of the
best ways my prospects and customers
can benefit from doing business with me?"
This is a slightly different way of asking the
same question they're asking themselves.

- -

Why prospects don't buy right away:

#1. Not enough pain with their current situation.

#2. They don't perceive they have a need.

#3. They can't distinguish that you're any better.

#4. They don't trust you, your company, or your offer.

#5. They don't trust themselves
or think it will work for them.

#6. You did not follow-up enough
or put enough pressure on them.

Notice how "not having the money" is not on the list?

Six steps to closing any sale:

#1. Establish your credibility. Convince them
that you are the expert who can help them
solve some of their biggest problems.

#2. Know your prospect in the most intimate way. What
are they really searching for? In a perfect world, if you
could give them anything they wanted, what would it be?

#3. Understand the main benefits your product or
service can give to the people who buy it. A benefit
is the end emotional result that someone can get
when they purchase your product or service. What are
the biggest and most important benefits of what you
sell and how they are different from similar items?

#4. Only sell concepts and benefits. Disclose the facts,
but put all of your emphasis on the main benefits of
whatever you're offering in exchange for their money.

#5. Communicate your enthusiasm, certainty, and
confidence in the strongest way. What people really
want is total certainty. They want to feel they can
fully trust you and that you have their best interests
at heart and will never let them down. The more you
can do to convince them of these things, the more sales,
easier sales, and bigger sales you will get! Selling is a
transference of belief and emotion. The more you can do
to become completely sold on whatever you're trying to
sell to them, the more power you will have to sell them.
Be passionate about what you sell and make them feel it!

#6. Tell them what they must do to order now, and make them an irresistible offer that eliminates any excuse to not give you their money! Don't ask for the sale, practically demand they give it to you! That sounds clever, I know. But this is the exact approach that many of the greatest salespeople use. As long as you have done the other steps the right way, then you have earned the right to firmly ask your prospective buyer to give you their money. Don't wimp out on this final step. This is what separates the big dogs from the whimpering puppies.

Do all you can to take the prospect through the above six steps. Then make them the most irresistible offer possible, and in a very nice, but firm way, tell them exactly what to do right now. Give them at least two options, and ask them which one they want. Don't let them think about it. Don't let them tell you they'll get back with you. Make them the best offer and let them know that tomorrow could be too late. Put the pressure on them while also assuring them that you have a no-risk guarantee that protects them fully.

- -

The natural law of sales:

Whenever something is easy to sell, no one (except an idiot!) is going to pay you a lot of money to sell it. The big bucks are paid to the salespeople who can bring in the toughest sales, that are almost impossible for weaker salespeople to make.

The price you pay.

Others can point you in the right direction, but there is no substitute for direct experience. You learn through doing. It takes awareness and practice to develop new knowledge and skills. The willingness to suffer a little to gain a lot is one of the most important success principles. You can have almost anything, if you want it bad enough and are willing to pay the price to get it.

That price includes a great deal of learning and practice to develop the skills, abilities, and resources that will ultimately take you where you want to go.

- -

Can you really demand that they give you their money? Yes!

When it comes to asking for the order, most salespeople are way too timid. The prospect senses this and backs off. Every salesperson asks for the order, but the sales superstars practically demand it. They ask for the order with a firm sense of conviction and an attitude of "likeable authority". This makes people feel very confident that they're making the right decision. Prospects respond to certainty and confidence. You must act the way they expect you to act. If not, you'll kill the sale.

The truth must be sugarcoated.
You can't tell people too much too
fast or you'll scare them away!

- -

From Tom Hopkins' phenomenal book,
"How to Master the Art of Selling":

"I learned a long time ago that selling is the highest paid
hard work and the lowest paid easy work, that I could find.
And I also found out another exciting thing about selling –
the choice was mine, all mine. By myself, I could make it
the highest paid hard work, or I could let it be the lowest paid
easy work. I discovered that what I'd achieve in my selling
career was entirely up to me, and that what anyone else
wanted wasn't going to make much difference. What anyone
else would or wouldn't give me wasn't going to make much
difference, either. The only thing that really mattered was
what I did for myself, and what I gave to myself.

Will you agree with me on that? I hope so, because
the whole point of this book is that the skills, knowledge,
and drive within you are what will make you great, and
that these qualities can be expanded and intensified,
if you're willing to invest time and effort and money in
yourself. Is there any better investment than in yourself?
Most of us know there isn't, but many of us don't act
often enough, or decisively enough, on that belief.

You are your greatest asset. Put your time, effort, and money
into training, grooming, and encouraging your greatest asset."

From my favorite movie, "Broadcast News":

"And try to punch one word or phrase in every sentence – punch one idea a story. Punch! … And remember – you're not just reading the news or narrating. Everybody has to sell a little. You're selling them this idea of you. You know, what you're sort of saying is, 'trust me. I'm, uh, credible.' So whenever you catch yourself just reading…stop and start selling a little."

- -

Differentiation.

Find items to compare what you sell with the things that are most familiar and important to your best prospects and customers. What's different about you and what you sell from all of the others? Create some powerful comparisons to help make your answer stronger and more compelling.

- -

Build your sales messages the same way an expensive defense attorney would go to work to get his or her billionaire client (who was on trial for murder!) from spending even one day in jail.

The wisdom of Claude Hopkins:

"He never sought to sell anything; instead he offered people 'the privilege of buying.' He did not say, "Buy my brand, not the other fellow's." Instead he said, "I will show you why it is better to buy from me, because I am doing you a favor." He thought that the most easily exploitable of all emotions was curiosity. His favorite maxim was: No argument can compete with one dramatic demonstration."
From the book "Taken at the Flood" by John Gunther

The above paragraph contains 2 great marketing ideas:

#1. The best way to sell is not to sell. That's what Educational Marketing is all about; you bring in new customers by trying to teach them something that's very important to them. This is the lure. Then, after they are convinced that you are the expert they should work with, you offer them the privilege of doing business with you.

#2. Look for ways to dramatize your offer. A dramatic demonstration can help you make sales when everything else failed. What can you do to highlight the major benefits of what you sell in the most compelling way?

- -

All the money is made in the follow-up.
The trick is to create a marketing system that keeps the pressure on them, so you don't have to.

Before you try to sell somebody else,
make sure you're 100% sold yourself.

Do your pre-game. Take a few moments and psych yourself
up! Motivate yourself! Plan. Prepare! Get your head in the
right frame of mind. Lift yourself up! Make sure you are
100% on fire! Because all selling is a transference of belief
and emotion, you will always make more sales, faster and
easier, by spending quality time re-selling yourself before
you open your mouth. And during this period of pumping
yourself up, remind yourself that you are helping your
prospect make a decision that will be perfect for them.
Convince yourself that your #1 mission is to help your target
prospect make the right decision. It sounds so simple and
it is! But many sales reps are only half sold on what they're
selling, and many veteran salespeople lose many sales
that should be theirs because they're not fully prepared
to play the game. The prospects feel these things and run.

- -

The 3-part sales process:

#1. Lead generation – Getting the largest number
of the most qualified buyers in your market to come
to you (so you'll never make a single cold call!).

#2. Education – Doing all you can to prove to
them that you can give them what they want.

#3. Closing – Making it easy for
them to do business with you.

The road to success is never straight or flat.
All growth is three steps forward and two
steps back. Accept this and keep pushing on!

- -

The ABC's of wealth.

I started my first business in 1985 and called it "ABC's Carpet
and Upholstery Cleaning". That name came from formula
called "the ABC's of success" in a book I was reading.

The formula went like this: All you need to make
your dreams come true is the right ATTITUDE, a strong
and unshakable BELIEF, and a firm COMMITMENT.
The author told me that if I had all three of these things I
could never fail! So, because I wanted to motivate myself in
the most passionate way, I made this my company name
and told everyone about the ABC's of success. I was like
a newborn Christian who was out to save the world!

But eventually I stopped believing in the ABC's formula.
I laughed at myself for believing such a shallow idea.
I learned so much about business and marketing.
I made a ton of money and felt sorry for those poor
"self-help addicts" who put their hope in silly acronyms.
I felt proud and superior. But now, several decades later,
I've come full circle. Now I see that the true secret
to success is in the right combination of specific
business building knowledge and skills, coupled
with something as simple as the ABC formula.

The #1 goal of your marketing system is to
get the right people to come to you pre-sold.

This is a better way to sell:

#1. It lets you reach the best prospects.

#2. It makes them feel as if they're seeking you out
(without you having to do any cold calling).

#3. It educates people about all the reasons why you (and
what you sell) is the ultimate solution they're looking for.

#4. The sale of a low cost initial product lets you pay
for some of your advertising and marketing expenses.

#5. This brings the best people to you... presold! The more
they read, watch, and listen to your materials, the more
they will sell themselves on why they must buy from you.

- -

We're living in a world where everyone is suspect, where nobody trusts anyone.

Thank God, there are exceptions! But until you win people's
trust, they will always hold back. They will always doubt
you and your intentions. They will always be somewhat
suspicious of what you say and do. Once you win
someone's trust, you can say and do almost anything
and it will be okay. But without their trust, every move
you make will be doubted, analyzed, and criticized.

The powerful need to feel superior.

The need to be superior is the driving force behind
all human behavior and yet almost nobody
will admit this. Most folks will never admit it,
but we tend to look for some way that we can
feel as if we are better than other people. The more
ambitious a person is, the more they tend to have
this powerful desire. How can you fill the powerful
need your prospects have to feel superior?

- -

Six principles of influence.

Persuasion is much more of a science than an art.
There are many principles of persuasion such as
these six that have been tested and proven to work:

#1. Reciprocation – We feel obligated to return
acts of kindness that others do for us.

#2. Authority – We look to experts to show us the way.

#3. Commitment/Consistency – We want to act
consistently with our commitments and values).

#4. Scarcity – Nobody wants something
that everyone else can have. The less

available the resource, the more we want it.

#5. Liking – The more we perceive that people are just like us, the more we want to say yes to them.

#6. Social Proof – We look to what others do to guide our behavior.

These persuasion principles were made famous by Robert Cialdini. Find as many ways as you can to add them to your sales and marketing.

- -

So what?

Who cares?

What's in it for me?

Those are the three things that people are unconsciously thinking as they're listening to your sales pitch.

- -

Do something every day that scares you.

This will stretch you beyond your comfort zone. That's what self-discipline is all about. It's pushing yourself to do the most important and most difficult things that lead to you getting the biggest results you want the most.

All of us are searching for the few who can and will
rather than the much larger group who can't or won't.

The key is to develop a marketing
system that does most of this for you.

- -

The #1 reason people buy a business opportunity...
The secret is in this quote by Charles Kingsley:

"We act as though comfort and luxury were the chief
requirements of life, when all that we need to make us
really happy is something to be enthusiastic about."

This is the key to selling business opportunities.
People are searching for something to feel excited about!
They want positive hope for the future, and this is
what they get when they buy a business opportunity.

- -

Obstacles are the things you see when
you take your eyes off your goals.

- -

The secret of success is
building your business around
the lifestyle you want to live.

The #1 reason most people don't promote
themselves as much as they could
and should is because they're worried
about what others will say or think.

Stop doing this! The only people who matter are the ones
who give you their money. Forget your peers, family,
competitors, and/or the community. You must promote
yourself even harder to attract and re-sell to the largest
number of the best prospective buyers in your marketplace.
These are the only people whose opinion matters.

- What can you do to prove that you
are the best choice for their money?

- How can you win their trust and respect?

- What can you do to earn a permanent
slot in their heads and hearts?

- How can you prove that you're the expert
who can take them where they want to go?

- -

The power of negative thinking.

Always assume that your prospect
doesn't believe a word you say.
Overcoming this negative premise is
the secret to achieving a positive result.

"Get them to see the worst and then sell them the insurance."

Those words were spoken by a man who sold millions of dollars worth of insurance. The lesson: You can't sell the solution until you help them to see the biggest problems that your product or service solves. So make it real. Personalize it for them. Try to make them fee the pain of the problem before you sell your solution.

- -

A lesson from Hollywood.

When asked how he dealt with the 14 years of drought in his career when nobody was calling and the parts he was offered sucked, John Travolta said, "I never stopped believing in myself, no matter what other people said about me or my future." This is brilliant! In fact, when I read this quote, I instantly recognized it as one of the most important qualities that all great entrepreneurs possess. Business is always up and down. There are times of feast and famine. Nobody survives long-term in any kind of major way, without working through some very dark times. These difficult times lay ahead on every entrepreneur's road to riches. During these hard times, you are tested in the most painful ways. You either break down or break through. You either let these terrible periods make or break you. These are the periods where you learn your greatest lessons and discover what's most important.

Getting their attention is never enough.

One of my friends was frustrated because he couldn't reach
me on the phone. This was in the late 1980s before cell
phones and my wife and I were on vacation. My friend
didn't know this. Instead, he thought the gatekeepers at
our office were not getting his repeated messages to me.
So after several days he became very frustrated and
left this message: "Tell T.J. I must get through to him.
My 7-year-old son just died and I must speak with him!"
Do you think that message got through? Yes, and fast!
Our staff went into overdrive. They knew that John and I were
good friends and they made a flurry of phone calls to track
my wife and I down and deliver this tragic news. And with
enough calls to enough people, the message did get to me.
I went into panic mode. So did Eileen. We raced to the
nearest phone and by the time I got through to him,
I was in a frantic state of mind. Then imagine my surprise
when he started laughing and told me it was just a joke.
Well, it certainly wasn't a joke to me. In fact, that day was
the beginning of the end of a long and important friendship.
Nothing was the same after that. Is there a marketing
lesson here? Yes. Here it is: you must get the
right people's attention, but it has to be done
in the right way or it will backfire on you.

- -

Get rid of the people who try so damn hard
to hold you back. And if you can't get rid
of them, ignore them. Don't give these
people the power to crush your dream.

13 questions to answer
in every sales presentation:

#1. Who are you?

#2. What do you do?

#3. How do you do it?

#4. Why should I listen to you?

#5. How are you different?

#6. Why do I need you?

#7. Who else have you helped?

#8. How long will it take?

#9. What if I'm not happy?

#10. How much will it cost?

#11. How do I know I can trust you?

#12. Why should I do this now?

#13. What's the worst that
can happen if I don't do it?

The hard times in life often tear you apart,
but don't give up and you'll grow back stronger.

- -

Information overload is the disease of the 21st Century.

Your prospects and customers are overwhelmed
and overloaded with too much information.
Many of them are skeptical and jaded. Trying to
give them more of it is not the answer. Their brains
are so full they can't take another idea! All of the
choices only confuse and frustrate them even more.
They need someone to ease their pain and make
complicated things seem simple. That's what you'll
do when you give them the right examples, stories,
concepts, and metaphors. This makes it easier
for them to understand the advantage you offer.

Many salespeople confuse information with communication.
They tell them too much, too fast. Instead, use stories,
examples, and metaphors to win their trust and build a
connection. Spoon feed your sales pitch to them and strive
to leave them wanting more. Create and build irresistible
offers that stack as many benefits as possible. Tell them
why you're willing to give them so much for so little.
And then follow it all up with a bold guarantee that
lets them feel as if they have more power than you do.

23 unconscious emotional desires that cause people to buy:

#1. People want hope for their future.

#2. They want to feel superior to others, or simply to feel better about themselves.

#3. They are searching for instant results.

#4. They want someone or something to believe in.

#5. They crave certainty.

#6. They're looking for someone to comfort or take care of them.

#7. They want peace and security.

#8. They dream of having more power and control!

#9. They love to be moved emotionally. To have something to get and stay excited about! And to feel deeply connected to something or someone they perceive as important.

#10. They love to be right and hate it when people make them feel as if they're wrong.

#11. Many are desperate to be an important part of something big and exciting!

#12. They want to feel wanted and needed.

#13. Older people want to re-experience some of the emotions they had when they were young.

#14. Most are looking for someone or something to show them the way.

#15. Many people these days want someone else to do it for them!

#16. They are looking for an easier way. They want all of the benefits without the time, work, risk, or high cost that others must pay or suffer through. In other words, they're looking for all the good without any of the bad.

#17. They want to be entertained! To have someone or something excite them!

#18. They are searching for something to take away their emotional pain.

#19. People love to have an enemy to fight against! They love the idea that all of the things that are wrong in their life are not their fault!

#20. To be young and free again.

#21. Many desperately want to feel loved and needed. They are desperate for some real appreciation. They want to feel special.

#22. They want to feel superior and dream of living the kind of life that others can only dream of.

#23. In a very unconscious way, they want immortality and many products and services (especially insurance!) fill this powerful need.

So consider the unconscious emotional needs and desires that cause your prospects and customers to buy. Get on the other side of the cash register and think like a marketer. Find the people who are doing the best job of reaching people emotionally. Study them. Learn what they have to teach. Try as hard as you can to remain as objective as possible, so you don't get caught up in the magic spell they cast on their subjects! Then strive to model their actions.

- -

The quality of your life and business is dependent on the quality of the people you surround yourself with.

Why some people can't sell
expensive products and services.

I know a brilliant marketer who has one major flaw: He can't sell expensive items and always wants to lower the price. All of his stuff is too damn cheap! And any time somebody wants to do a joint venture deal with him, all he wants to do is cut the price in order to "stimulate sales." This drives me crazy! Why? Because I fully expect this kind of behavior from a weak or inexperienced marketer, but not from a veteran and certainly not from someone as brilliant as my friend.

All of this has puzzled me greatly. Why does someone who knows how important it is to charge premium prices, and who has many competitors who are getting the big bucks find it impossible to charge more money? This mystified me for years. And then the answer hit me like a bolt of lightning! I was listening to one of Grant Cardone's audio CDs when he made a statement that almost caused me to drive off the road. Here it is: "Salespeople who are super frugal and count every dollar and weigh every decision by how much it will cost, will never be able to sell premium priced items." That blew me away! There was the answer to my burning question. You see, my brilliant marketing friend is one of the most frugal people on the planet! He is focused on the cost of everything. He's one of the most cost-conscious people I've ever met. He is totally focused on the cost of every aspect of his business and loves to negotiate. And yet, the same skills that make him a highly effective negotiator also makes it impossible to ask for and receive premium prices for the products and services he sells. Because he is so focused on what everything costs, he naturally thinks his buyers feel the same exact way.

You can never know the real value of
one thing until and unless you have
something else to compare it with or against.

Use comparisons to educate your customers and prospects
on all the ways that you, your company, and/or your
products and services are the right choice for them.
Help them understand why they must buy what you
sell by comparing it to something of great value to the
people in your market. It's up to you to make it real.

- -

People who are looking for
excuses will find them everywhere.

But the more committed you are, the less excuses
you'll make. Nothing can stop you! Nothing will get in
your way. No matter what the obstacle, you'll find a way
around it, under it, or through it! A wise person once said,
"Apathy will always find an excuse, but love will always
find a way." It's true. The deeper and more passionately
you believe in something and love it with all your heart,
the more you'll do to fight for it. You'll be fully committed.
Nothing will get in your way. Nothing will cause you
to lose your focus. You will be totally relentless.
You'll be on a mission and you won't stop until
you win! This mindset, along with a complete
understanding of all aspects of sales and
marketing and the willingness to do whatever
it takes, will make you an unstoppable!

From $700,000 a year
to delivering pizza.

I saw a story on some news program about an ex-salesman from Florida who was making as much as $700,000 a year, less than four years ago, and is now a pizza delivery driver. The media loves these stories. The producers of ABC's "20-20" probably crapped all over themselves when they stumbled onto that one!

It made me sick. I was disgusted and angry. The producers tried hard to paint a sad picture of this miserable man and his family who had been at the very top a handful of years ago and had now lost everything. It was embarrassing and humiliating to put this couple on national TV, talking about all kinds of personal things, in front of millions of people, but that's what the media does.

Anyway, that's not the part of the story that upset me so greatly. What made me so angry was:

> #1. The man who was making as much
> as $700,000 a year had one of the
> best educations that money could buy.

#2. He knew how to sell, but wasn't using his sales skills.

The world is filled with people who are not doing a damn thing with their college education. This is stupid, and yet I have met so many people with great educations who are doing nothing with them, that it barely phases me. I dropped out of high school and went to work. I had many meaningless low skilled jobs until I learned how to sell and started my own business. Anyway, one of my first jobs was working on a landscaping crew. I was a 16-year-old high school dropout and one of the guys on my crew was 10 years older than me and had just graduated from college with a Masters Degree. This guy was working right beside me and only getting $1.00 more per hour. I was shocked! He spent 8 years in college and was only making one dollar an hour more than I was!

But what bothered me the most about the man in my Florida story was the fact that he was a salesman in his former job, that's how he was making up to $700,000 in one year. But he probably didn't even think of himself as a salesman. In his minimum-wage-pizza-delivery-mind, he was a "Financial Broker" and he was "taking care of his clients' portfolios", or something like that. He thought of himself as "a highly educated and skilled professional" and not some kind of "salesperson." And yet that's exactly what he was! His income was tied to the amount of volume he produced. He may have been working for some prestigious financial institution, but to me he was simply a high paid salesperson. The only real problem, when I say he was a highly paid salesman, I mean it as a compliment, and someone like him probably thought of this in the lowest way.

It bothers me that selling has a such a bad rap. I am proud to be a salesperson. Selling is a noble profession. The world's most successful people are all great salespeople. They know how to electrify people with their words and actions! They know how to influence people and make them want to do whatever they want.

And perhaps above all else: they know how to create money where no money existed before. That's the greatest skill of every great salesperson. It's that kind of skill this man former stockbroker salesman in Florida had, and yet he was too blind to see it. Now he was doing the kind of job that any 15-year-old kid can do, when he could be making a ton of money with his sales skills.

Do you have to lie?

All salespeople must walk the razor's edge. If we tell the whole truth upfront, we'll scare our best prospects into the arms of our competitors. If we don't tell them enough of the truth, then we're being dishonest. Most prospects can't handle the entire truth before they buy. The reality behind what we sell will always be loaded with good and bad. However, the only thing most prospects want to hear about is the good. They're afraid of losing their money or getting into something they can't get out of.

Here's how to solve this problem:

• Sell them what they want and give them what they need. You wouldn't start a newborn baby out on solid food because there's no way their digestive system can handle it. The same is true of new customers. They can't handle the entire truth at first. So don't talk too much about the down side until they buy an initial low cost product or service from you. Then spoon-feed the truth to them a little at a time.

• Don't run them off! You can't take someone from A to Z overnight. You must move them through the truth-telling process slowly. If you try to tell people too much too fast, you'll scare them away. So you must have some type of process that slowly reveals things to them at a pace they're comfortable with. What is the real truth anyway? Oftentimes it is multi-faceted and subjective. There are usually many different sides to every issue. Because of this, you have to show them the side of the truth that won't scare them away.

• Give them small doses of reality. Shocking people with small doses of the truth makes them trust you and opens the door to other important aspects of your sales pitch.
    This wakes them up like a hard slap in the face!
For example, the first time I met my printer, I asked him the same question every new prospect asks: "Can you give me the best price?" And without hesitation, Steve said, "Sometimes YES, and sometimes NO!" This got my attention because I wasn't expecting it! Then he began to educate me about all of the things that made his company different than all the others and why he couldn't always give me the best price on every type of job. Another example:
Many of my clients want to make millions of dollars in a few short years like my wife and I did. So during our events, I like to get them excited about this burning desire and convince them that they really can do it! I hype it up! I get them all fired up! Then I drop the truth bomb: I tell them that "if they want to make millions of dollars" they must be

willing to put up with a lot of million-dollar headaches. This takes some of the excitement away, but now they can begin to understand some of the other things they need to know.

• Sell against the enemy. You can tell people the truth once you convince them that a major part of the problems they are facing is because someone else (or a group of others) have lied to them. Now you take them out of the equation. The reason for their problem is somebody else's fault and you become the good guy who is there to rescue them!

- -

Is all of this manipulative? You bet! But selling is manipulation.

Let me tell you another story. One of my suppliers is an awesome salesman. One day he was trying to convince me to do something (selling) and he began a sentence with "To tell you the truth..." I interrupted him and said, "Does that mean that you don't always tell me the truth?" to which he replied "YES!" And then, without missing a beat, he went back into his pitch! The reason he was able to tell me that he doesn't always tell me the truth and still get more of my business is because I trust him. He can say anything to me and never has to worry. This gives him the freedom to tell me the truth without any sugarcoating. But because I trust him, there can also be plenty of times when he keeps certain things away from me and/or puts some kind of positive spin on something, without telling me everything. Once you win people's trust, you'll have that kind of leverage.

Unreasonable people rule the world.

Those who are most committed make the biggest impact. They're on fire! It's easy to spot these people and impossible to stop them. They're movers and shakers. They're freaks and fanatics! They're the ones who will move heaven and earth to get what they want and make it happen. Were they born this way? No! You can become more unreasonable, right now! Just strive to become much more passionate and enthusiastic about your life (and sales career!) and even more determined to get what you want. Here's how:

A. It starts with your decision and commitment to be, do, and have more of the best things that life has to offer.

B. It's your total dedication to achieve your biggest goals, dreams, and desires, no matter what.

C. It's understanding the price you have to pay to get what you want. Then it's your willingness and ability to continue to pay that price, no matter the cost.

D. It's your refusal quit.

E. It's your fighting spirit! This will make it easier to get back up every time you get knocked down.

F. It's not caring what anyone thinks about you.

G. It's the full expression of who you are. Your willingness to make a complete fool of yourself, rather than holding back!

Anybody can do these things. The fact that so few do is a great mystery to me.

Who's fault is it if your sales are not high enough?

Every salesperson wants to take the credit when their sales are high. But when their sales begin to suffer, those same people will start to blame everyone and everything else.

It's easy to make excuses when things get bad. For many years I told people that I was 100% responsible for my success or lack of success, and yet my attitude sucked! I wasn't fully committed. I blamed other people and situations for my business related problems. When things went wrong, I'd cry and whine like a big baby! I created elaborate stories in my head about why my sales were so low and why things weren't working out. What I should have done is focused on all of the things I could do to get out of these problems and then put all of my creative power into making more sales!

- -

How to make people trust you.

Getting people to drop their guard and trust you is the key to making more sales, faster and easier. The secret is to be 100% genuine. Strive to discover your own unique energies and desires, and find your own way to express yourself. When you do that, you won't be following the follower. You won't be trying to live up to an image that was laid on you by society, family, tradition, or the people around you. You'll be on the path of full self-expression and this will make you totally unique. People will not always like you, but most of them will respect you. They'll sense that you really are different. You're not being fake and phony. You're not holding back. Once they sense this about you, you will begin to win their trust.

The people we admire the most are following their own path. They listen to their own inner voice. They move in their own direction. They question authority, question tradition, question the rules, and have no fear of how others perceive them. These people have found freedom in an unfree world. There's something about them that inspires our trust. They attract others to them because they're true-blue originals who dance to the beat of a different kind of drummer. They are real, raw, honest, and totally different. They are a refreshing change in a sea of nameless faceless robotic people and this makes others want to be around them and do business with them.

It takes great courage to be authentic.
To be totally real. To express yourself fully.
And yet this is the way to win the trust and respect of the people you want to attract and sell to.

- -

Selling is a type of performance art.

It's all about your presentation and the unique way you dramatize your offer. It's how you make your biggest claims. It's the way you make it exciting! All this can and should be elevated to a form of art.

Let me tell you one of
my favorite sales stories.

It's Saturday morning and this guy I've never seen
knocks on our door with a clip board in his hand.
I look him over and think he might be from the
government or something. "Maybe this is important?"
I thought. I hated the fact that he was knocking on
our door on a Saturday morning, but I walked out on
the porch to try to get rid of him as fast as possible...

An hour later, he walked away with $18,000.

Did he stick a gun in my face?

No... He sold me and my wife!

Here's the rest of the story: The guy and his son want to seal
or/or pave our huge driveway. We've had this done before
and it's never worked out. In fact, the last few times we let
someone do this have been very disappointing. We couldn't
even get some of these people to come back and fix their
mistakes. So I tell him all of this, say 'thanks, but no
thanks!' and began to walk back into the house.

But this guy is a great salesman. Real low key. He comes
across as very honest and sincere. So I agreed to let him
and his son measure our driveway. I thought we'd let him
give us a bid and then I'd get rid of him. He thanks me
and I go back into the house. But now I'm watching from

the window as he and his son begin to put on a real show. They acted like measuring our driveway was rocket science! They both moved very slow and acted so serious. They made a ton of calculations on their clip boards (they were probably scribbling dollar signs!). I'm watching all of this and knew that everything they were doing was part of their "sales presentation", and yet I loved it!

They finally get done and I prepare myself for a great sales pitch. He doesn't disappoint me. He begins to tell my wife and I what he thinks is the best idea for fixing all of the holes in our driveway "for the least amount of money". He tells us why his solution is what we need. Then he shoots us a per square foot price that seems dirt-cheap! That "dirt-cheap" price turns out to be $18,000 when the entire job is calculated...

Then came our objections. Eileen and I threw four or five fast concerns and he handled each one in the same honest low-key way. "This guy is good!" I thought. But then I started to feel pressured because I didn't want to spend $18,000 and I was beginning to believe what he and his son were telling us. So I threw one last big objection that went like this: "What happens if we have a problem after you've done the job?" He paused for a minute. Then he looked at his son and both of them smiled and said, "Just give us a call!" They said those same five words at the same time! It was like listening to a choir! They even talked alike! As soon as they did that, they had our money.

Be relentless in your follow-up, because:

#1. Good prospects love to be chased. This makes
them feel important. As long as you follow-up in the
most passionate way, from a sincere and altruistic
position, and assuming they really are qualified
prospects, you almost can't follow-up enough.

#2. It can take a lot of follow up marketing to get the sale.

Here's a great visual analogy:

Picture yourself chopping down a big tree. You want
your axe to be as sharp as possible. But it may take
a couple of hundred hits before the tree falls. Each blow
gets you closer to chopping down the tree. And yet,
in the beginning it will seem as if nothing's happening.
Can you see this? I hope so! Just picture yourself
chopping away, working up a major sweat, but nothing
is happening. The same thing happens when you
follow-up with good prospects. Each new follow-up
is a swing of the axe! You must keep chopping
away at their sales resistance until they fall.

- -

The single greatest word
in the English language.

This word is "why". Ask yourself why the things you want are
so important. What's behind the goals you want to achieve?

What are you really searching for? What's the real desire behind your biggest desires? The clearer you are about the "Why?" your goals are so important, then the more motivation you'll have. So answer these questions:

- What's most important to you and why?

- Why do your goals mean so much to you?

The right "why" to do something will empower you to create the "how" to do it. So spend a lot of time thinking through the "whys". Dig deeper. Think!

That leads to the next greatest word which is "how". The secret: "Why?" leads to "How?" The question "Why?" creates the demand. "How?" you ultimately do it fills the demand. One reason many people fail to achieve their biggest goals is because they're too focused on how they're going to pull something off instead of the why it's so important in the first place.

- -

A goal setting secret that works:

Spend less time thinking about your goals and more time thinking and writing about your intentions. Intentions come before goals. They are the reasons why the goals you set for yourself are so important. The more time you spend thinking and writing about your intentions, the more motivation you'll have to achieve your goals.

14 essential questions:

#1. Do you have a genuine interest and passion for your market and the products and services you sell?

#2. Why do you want to sell to the people in your target market?

#3. How can you reach and sell to these people?

#4. Will these people buy from you long-term... How do you know?

#5. What products and services are most attractive to them?

#6. What is your major competitive advantage that sets you apart?

#7. What is the most profitable way to reach and sell to your market?

#8. Are they already buying the kinds of products and services you want to sell?

If so, what are the main strategies and methods that others are using to sell these items? How can you duplicate the best methods they're using?

#9. What are the top-3 reasons that the people in your target market will want to continue to do business with you?

#10. How will you re-sell the largest percentage of your best customers, for the largest profit per transaction?

#11. What are your biggest strengths and weaknesses?

How can you become even stronger in the areas of you are
already strong in and delegate all of your weakest areas?

#12. How much money do you want and why?

#13. Who are your 3 biggest or best competitors?

What are they doing right and
wrong? How can you beat them?

#14. What will you do if your grand
plans fail? What is your back-up plan?

The person who thinks everything
through in the most creative way,
sees it as a game, and plays to win,
will always be more successful.
Business is brutal. The markets
are constantly changing, and there
will always be new problems and
challenges that work against you,
if you're not on top of your game.
So play to win, but know that losing is
part of winning; so take your blows
and beatings and continue
to get back up to fight!

How I sold myself on 3 very important things and how you can, too:

#1. Happiness.

I spent years searching for happiness in all of the wrong places; always believing it was out there somewhere. It wasn't. It's been inside of me the whole time, fully within my power. The same is true for you: your ultimate happiness and feelings of deep satisfaction are gifts that only you can give to yourself. So take full responsibility for your own well-being. Your happiness is up to you. Once you accept that premise, you can create your own happiness that is completely independent of other people, places, and things.

#2. Health.

Back in the mid 1990s I realized that exercise is the best medicine. Today I believe it more than ever. And yet, the funny thing about exercise is the fact that, like happiness, nobody can do it for you.

#3. Financial independence.

I sold myself on the idea that I am the only one who can make myself financially independent. Other people are vital to my success, and yet, my continued ability to attract and retain the very best people I can find is the key to my own financial independence. It's your key, too.

Giving these gifts to yourself can be so hard. It's much easier to stay dependent, blame others, and make all kinds of excuses. But you don't have to do this. Just think all of this through and start giving yourself the ultimate gifts that only you can give to yourself.

- -

There's no such thing as non-manipulative selling.

All selling is manipulation, but we don't want to think of ourselves as manipulators. However, my dictionary defines manipulation as: "to manage or influence skillfully, especially in an unfair manner." Well that definition describes what selling is all about. My dictionary has four definitions for the word manipulation. I gave you the most controversial one because it ended with "in an unfair manner".

But what's unfair?

- Is it fair that todays buyer seems to resist everything we say and do?

- Is it fair that many of our prospects lie to us?

- Are people being fair with us when they make excuses of why they can't listen to what we have to say?

• Is it fair when even the best buyers
won't return our phone calls?

No way, Jose! None of this is fair to us, especially when we sell products and services that can make a real difference in peoples lives and all we're trying to do is give them what we know they really want. And some prospects go way beyond being unfair with us; they yell, scream, and curse at us.

None of this is fair.

So don't buy into the idea that there is a non-manipulative way to sell. That's nonsense! Selling is a game. It's a contest. A test of wills. It's your job to skillfully influence your prospects to buy from you instead of all the other people who are also trying to influence them. Fairness does not exist. Here's proof: My dictionary defines "fair" as: "Free from bias and dishonesty." Another definition is: "Free from blemish, imperfection, or anything that impairs the appearance, quality, or character." Wow! Once you grasp that meaning you will truly know that fairness in the marketplace is a myth.

I hate the sales trainers who teach what they call "non-manipulative selling". They want you to believe that selling is not a game, battle, war, or a test of wills between you and your prospect. They teach all this to make themselves look like the good guy in a wild west world of greedy manipulators. Ironically enough, most of the methods these sales trainers' teach are extremely manipulative! For example, their books and courses teach you how to make your prospective buyer feel that you truly care about them in the deepest sort of way so you can sell and re-sell to them with no resistance. What's non-manipulative about that?

In summary, the methods for persuading and influencing can be used for good or bad. You should strive to care about the people you do business with. Build bonds of trust with these people and give them what they want the most. But never think that anything you're doing to sell and re-sell them is non-manipulation. It's all pure manipulation and all the very best salespeople are all master manipulators. However, we use our skills in the most positive ways for the greater good of everyone we do business with.

SPECIAL ENDING

An Opportunity
and a Guarantee.

Thank you for reading my book.

By now you know, so much of what you've been taught about selling is wrong. Especially if you learned from a traditional sales training school or some old-school sales manager. For example, the days of HIGH-PRESSURE and overtly manipulative methods are over.

Those old-fashioned selling methods don't work any more... and that's a great thing! People refuse to be sold these days. They have way more natural sales resistance. Their "BS Radar" is hyper-active. And why shouldn't it be? They're been pitched 1,000 times by 1,000 slick salespeople. The old-world, high-pressure methods only make prospects want to run.

And I say... "Thank God for that!"

But here's the undeniable truth: Nobody makes money until something is sold. People must buy your product or service, before you can get paid. Even a trip to your local Walmart was often preceded by some kind of sales message that helps to determine what brand you decided to buy.

But wait a minute. If "sales" has to happen before money can be made... and if people refuse to subject themselves to the old-school high-pressure sales tactics of yesteryear... then how are you supposed to try to make sales these days?

The solution: What you need is a whole new approach to selling, like the methods you've read about in this book. This gives you a way to get people's attention, pre-sell the prospective buyers, and make them want to buy. This is a way to make more sales, without the high-pressure methods that don't work anymore. You can <u>fully automate</u> your entire sales process to make more sales, faster and easier! And that's good news, because now...

WE CAN HELP YOU DO IT!

Our **NO-PRESSURE SALES SYSTEM Coaching and Consulting Service** will help you use our powerful but little-known strategies. Let us send you a complete information package that shows you how these methods can help you get an almost unfair advantage over your competition. Our methods will push you ahead of other sales reps who still cling to the tired OLD-FASHIONED SELLING METHODS that <u>don't</u> work in today's marketplace. And if you manage a team, we can help your entire team learn these no-pressure secrets that can end up putting more money in your pocket!

These methods and strategies will change your life. Our NO-PRESSURE SALES SYSTEM is the only way to sell in today's world. It will change your entire approach to sales, selling, and doing business. You'll make more sales and, perhaps for the first time ever, you may actually enjoy selling!

We teach our NO-PRESSURE SALES SYSTEM as part of a coaching and consulting model. As a Member, you'll get access to core training resources, as well as ongoing coaching and consulting to help you master the art of making more sales with less pressure.

This book gave you some of my very best ideas. Now I want to invite you to become a Client of our **NO-PRESSURE SALES SYSTEM Coaching and Consulting Service**. Get back with me or my Affiliate who gave you this book. Let me or my Affiliate know that you'd like to know more about our Coaching and Consulting Service. I <u>promise</u> I'm ready, willing, and able to help you master these simple strategies to get more sales ... without using any high-pressure tactics. I <u>guarantee</u> these secrets will help you make more sales and profits. I look forward to sending you more information and (hopefully) welcoming you as a Client. Thanks again for reading my book. Please let me hear from you right away!

www.ingramcontent.com/pod-product-compliance
Lightning Source LLC
Chambersburg PA
CBHW032006190326
41520CB00007B/378